Successful
Career Planning
in a week

Wendy Hirsh and
Charles Jackson

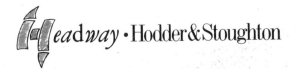
Headway · Hodder & Stoughton

British Library Cataloguing in Publication Data

A catalogue record for this title is available from
the British Library

ISBN 0 340 59855 7

First published 1994
Impression number 10   9   8   7   6   5   4
Year   1999   1998   1997

Typeset by Multiplex Techniques Ltd, St Mary Cray, Kent.
Printed in Great Britain for Hodder & Stoughton
Educational, a division of Hodder Headline Plc, 338 Euston
Road, London NW1 3BH by Cox & Wyman Ltd, Reading,
Berkshire.

the Institute of Management

F O U N D A T I O N

The Institute of Management (IM) is at the forefront of management development and best management practice. The Institute embraces all levels of management from students to chief executives. It provides a unique portfolio of services for all managers, enabling them to develop skills and achieve management excellence.

For information on the benefits of membership, please contact:

Department HS
Institute of Management
Cottingham Road
Corby
Northants NN17 1TT

Tel. 01536 204222
Fax 01536 201651

This series is commissioned by the Institute of Management Foundation.

CONTENTS

■ I N T R O D U C T I O N ■

Work is an important part of our lives. We rely on it for income, but many of us also want more. We expect work to be interesting, to use our skills, and to fit in with our other commitments and interests. We often seek a sense of moving forward in our working lives. This is what many people mean by the term 'career'.

However, very few of us put much effort into planning for the kind of career we want. Thinking about where we are going at work is something we all need to do throughout our working lives.

By working through a simple series of steps and exercises, you can help yourself to be clear about what you want, what your options are, and how to move forward. If you want to use this book to go through these steps, you should begin by acquiring a notebook or folder in which to keep the information you will be generating.

We shall look at one step in this process of career planning on each day of the week:

Sunday	What do you want from work?
Monday	What kind of job would you enjoy?
Tuesday	What are you good at?
Wednesday	Identifying your career options
Thursday	Collecting information
Friday	Making a choice
Saturday	Taking the first steps

What do you want from work?

In taking the first steps towards a new career plan, we look at the following issues:

- your motivation for planning
- a simple framework for career planning
- what you want from work

As we set out to consider what we are doing at work and where we wish to go, there are always a number of seemingly good reasons to put it off yet again. So we have to start by confronting why we need to look at our own careers, and what the likely benefits might be.

Clearing away the barriers

The very term 'career' can seem daunting. It sounds like an ever-upward march to a predetermined senior job. In fact, careers are simply sequences of job experiences. They often involve sideways moves, moves between employers and/or between different types of work, and periods out of paid employment altogether. Such careers need thinking about if we are to find satisfaction in the combination of our work and non-work lives.

A barrier to career planning for many people is the lack of a clear approach to thinking their way through the many uncertainties involved in sorting out future job options. We will introduce a simple framework which can be used to guide our thinking.

Once you have looked at why you need to plan and understood the overall framework, then you are ready to move on to the first personal task: to take a long cool look at what you really want to get out of work.

The aim of these initial steps is to reduce your level of anxiety and set you free to think as widely as possible before you narrow down the field to particular jobs. Few of us are ever really lateral enough in our career planning.

Why try to plan your career?

Most of us feel from time to time that we should reconsider where we are going, but it seems safer not to think about it just yet.

Career planning is not just for the very young or the redundant. Most of us will need to rethink our careers several times in our working lives.

Such rethinking may lead to very modest changes, such as a rather different job with your current employer. Or it may

lead to much more radical change of direction, as you realise that the essence of your line of work does not suit or satisfy you. Or it may result in no change at all, except a new appreciation of where you are going and why it feels right.

Planning as a necessity
It is important to be aware that by not planning you put yourself in real danger.

Work opportunities are changing all the time, and some jobs become obsolete or reduce in numbers as others open up. If we do not ensure our own employability by acquiring the right skills and moving into areas which offer some opportunity, then no one else will do it for us.

Even for the person who stays within one organisation, gone are the days when careers were an orderly progression managed by the employer. These days more employers are expecting individual employees to take the main responsibility for their own careers. This means we must

look around for suitable job avenues to pursue and persuade our employers that we can tackle fresh challenges.

If you are in any real doubt as to whether you should stop and think about your career direction, remember that 'failing to plan is planning to fail'. Successful people often say they have 'just been lucky'. This is true only to the extent that none of us can map out our future careers in every detail. Success, however, does depend on having some goals in mind and seeking opportunities to move towards them.

Your own reasons for reviewing your career
Now you need to clarify why you are looking at your career at this particular time. Some reasons might be:

- not enjoying the current job (finding it boring, stressful, frustrating, etc.)
- feeling that career progression is blocked (no obvious next step, employer does not recognise potential etc.)

- suspicion that you are in the wrong kind of work altogether and need a more radical change
- fear of job loss, e.g. employer cutting jobs
- trying to find a new route back into paid work (after redundancy or a long period of caring for dependants)
- a desire for other forms of work (voluntary work, work in 'retirement', self-employment, etc.)
- wishing to find a better fit between work and non-work priorities (caring for children, less travelling, etc.)

A framework for career planning

Any approach to career planning involves focusing both on yourself and on the job market. The framework used here encourages you to think first about yourself.

First consider three main questions in relation to yourself:

- What do you want from work? (work values)
- What kind of job would you enjoy? (job interests)
- What are you good at? (skills)

Then turn your attention to the *job market* and:

- look at the broad types of jobs available
- identify some possible career options
- find out about jobs with which you are not familiar, either inside your organisation or elsewhere

On the firm foundation of these two types of knowledge you can then:

- make your career choice
- start to take action

A simple diagram can help you to remember these basic building blocks of career planning.

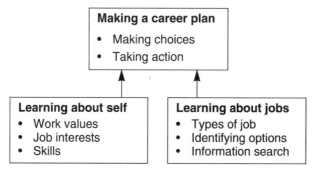

The building blocks of career planning

Making a career plan
- Making choices
- Taking action

Learning about self
- Work values
- Job interests
- Skills

Learning about jobs
- Types of job
- Identifying options
- Information search

What do you want to get out of work?

The rest of today's programme will be devoted to starting to look at what you really want from work: your *work values*.

You may feel you work primarily to pay the bills. However, if you had to choose between two similar jobs, would you automatically take the job which paid more? Not necessarily. One job might involve a longer journey to work, the other might be in an organisation you know to be facing an uncertain future.

It is clear that what would matter most to another person might not matter most to you. Some of us are happy to take

Cont. on p.14

Exercise 1: understanding your work values

Give each statement a score out of 10 using the scale below.

0   10

Not important   *Extremely important*
to me   *to me*

How important is it that your work:	Score
1 Encourages accomplishment and achievement?	....
2 Offers steady employment and security?	....
3 Provides recognition and prestige?	....
4 Involves risk and uncertainty?	....
5 Provides high financial rewards?	....
6 Benefits the community or provides a service to others?	....
7 Gives you the opportunity to use your initiative?	....
8 Is in an organisation that treats people fairly?	....
9 Is with colleagues that are easy to get along with?	....
10 Provides opportunities to lead and direct other people?	....

Now identify which statement has been given the highest
score and rank that statement 1, find the statement with the
next highest score and rank that statement 2, and so on. The
order in which the values have been ranked gives us
information about the kind of rewards we want from work.
Values ranked highest tell us about work settings that are
likely to be attractive to us and values ranked low are likely
to be unattractive to us.

Value	Work involves:	Rank
Achievement/ Challenge	Making use of our abilities; offering interest and challenge	....
Security/ Stability	A work environment that is comfortable and not stressful	....
Status	Economic, occupational or social standing; having an important role	....
Risk	Financial uncertainty, lack of job security, or physical danger	....
Economic	High salary	....
Altruism/ Service	Concern for the welfare of others	....
Autonomy/ Independence	Being in control of your own work	....
Equity	Concern for fairness and equality of opportunity at work	....
Social	Friendly work environment	....
Authority	Opportunities to manage and supervise; leadership	....

a risky career decision, because, for instance, we are confident in our own abilities, or because we think that a particular job is really worthwhile.

Start with your real priorities
Knowing the kind of work that would meet your real priorities means understanding your work values.

Start by completing Exercise 1 on pages 12–13.

Where does work fit with the rest of your life?
This is another key question to think about early in the career planning process. For example, how much time do you want to devote to work? It is not just a question of whether you want to to work full time or part time, or whether you mind working shifts or at weekends. The question is about how central you want your work to be in your life.

How important is it that you:

- Have opportunities to work as a 'volunteer' for a charity or in a political campaign?
- Spend time with your family and friends?
- Are involved in caring for children or elderly parents?
- Play sport or participate in your favourite hobby?

Perhaps it does not even matter if your work takes over the whole of your life, because what you plan to do is going to be so important to you.

It is not for ever
We all change, and our circumstances change. You are not committing yourself irreversibly to a course of action when you make career plans.

If you no longer want to continue with the sort of work you have been doing, it does not mean you were wrong to start doing this sort of work in the first place.

What matters most to someone at the age of 20 is not necessarily going to be what matters most to the same person at the age of 30 or 40. On the other hand, there may be things that you have always wanted to do or to try out but, for some reason, in the past have never had the opportunity to do or never thought it would be possible for them to be the basis of paid employment.

It is not too late
It may not be easy to change career direction, especially if it means leaving a well-paid secure job to start again at the bottom rung of a career ladder, or becoming a student again; but lots of people have done it.

Over the next six days we will work through the remaining six steps in planning your career. We continue on Monday by looking at job interests.

Summary

We have spent Sunday examining the crucial issue of what we want from work. In doing that we have looked at:

- the barriers to career planning
- why you need to plan your career
- your own reasons for reviewing your career
- a framework for career planning
- understanding your work values
- where work fits with the rest of your life

What kind of job would you enjoy?

Jobs differ in a wide variety of ways. Today we focus on trying to identify the sort of work that you would find interesting. Forget whether you have the skills, the knowledge, or even the experience; concentrate on finding out what kinds of work you would *enjoy*.

In doing this you are continuing with the process of learning about yourself. This is the essential first step to career planning. You may feel you already have a pretty good idea of what your interests are, but even if this is the case, there are several reasons why it is worth spending some time reviewing your interests. In particular, it is possible that those interests may have changed since you last thought about them. It is also helpful to be able to articulate your interests, especially when you start getting interviews for jobs. One of the favourite questions of job interviewers is, 'Why are you interested in this job?'

The map of work interests

Having got some idea about what is important to you, you need to start thinking about the direction in which you want to go. However, when embarking on any journey a map is required to show us what is out there. It is just the same when planning a career, although in this case several maps are required. Today, we are going to be looking at the first of these maps. This map is called *work interests*.

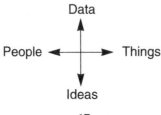

The first thing to do with any map is to orient it, and to do this we need a compass. The four points of the compass on the map of work interests are data, ideas, people and things.

The contents of jobs vary in many ways but some of the most fundamental differences concern whether they involve dealing with people, things, data or ideas. Of course, many types of work combine these four elements in varying proportions.

How to use the map

This map of work interests has several uses. First of all, if you are currently working, you can try to locate yourself, that is, to find out in what area of the map you are now. On the other hand, if you are not working at the present time you need to find out where you were on the map when you last worked. You also need to decide whether this is where you want to be or whether you really want to be somewhere else. Where would you like to be in an ideal world?

Once you have some firm ideas about where you want to be, you need to find out what sort of work opportunities exist there.

The problem is that there are so many jobs, and even the same job can seem quite different in one setting from how it feels in another. At this stage you are only trying to identify the territory in which you would like to be. Tomorrow you will have to determine whether you have, or can develop, the skills to survive there.

Establishing preferences: types of work activity

To help you determine what your work interests are, carry out the two exercises that follow. These look at interests in relation to six different types of work activity which combine a focus on people, things, data and ideas in various ways. The activities are:

- *Entrepreneurial* – activities found in business and management jobs
- *Administrative* – activities found in administrative and organisational jobs
- *Practical* – activities found in technical and practical jobs
- *Intellectual* – activities found in scientific and research jobs
- *Creative* – activities found in artistic and creative jobs
- *Social* – activities found in social and personal services jobs

The diagram shows how these six sorts of work activities relate to the two dimensions of our map: people – things and data – ideas.

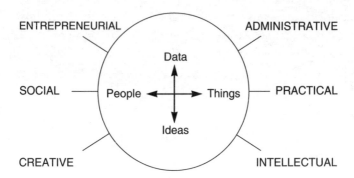

Exercise 2: your work interests

For the six sets of statements set out below, ask yourself:

'How interested am I in work that involves . . .'

Circle one number alongside each activity using the scale from 1 = no interest to 5 = strong interest

Entrepreneurial (data/people)

1 2 3 4 5   Persuading and influencing other people
1 2 3 4 5   Making business decisions
1 2 3 4 5   Managing/leading people
1 2 3 4 5   Taking business and financial risks
1 2 3 4 5   Getting people interested/involved in a project

Administrative (data/things)

1 2 3 4 5   Using a computer
1 2 3 4 5   Organising a filing system
1 2 3 4 5   Working with figures
1 2 3 4 5   Getting all the details right
1 2 3 4 5   Clear structure and routine

Practical (things)
1 2 3 4 5   Working with tools/machinery
1 2 3 4 5   Fixing and repairing things
1 2 3 4 5   Good hand-eye coordination
1 2 3 4 5   Working outside
1 2 3 4 5   Developing practical skills

Intellectual (ideas/things)
1 2 3 4 5   Understanding/being curious
1 2 3 4 5   Researching/analysing information
1 2 3 4 5   Asking questions
1 2 3 4 5   Solving problems in your own way
1 2 3 4 5   Learning about new things

Creative (people/ideas)
1 2 3 4 5   Using your imagination/expressing your ideas
1 2 3 4 5   Designing and making things
1 2 3 4 5   Performing/participating in artistic activities
1 2 3 4 5   Watching plays, films/listening to music
1 2 3 4 5   Working alongside creative people

Social (people)
1 2 3 4 5   Teaching people
1 2 3 4 5   Helping people with their problems
1 2 3 4 5   Meeting and talking to people
1 2 3 4 5   Building relationships with people
1 2 3 4 5   Looking after and caring for people

Add up the score for each set of items (maximum score for each area is 25). Then list in your notebook the six types of activity in rank order from rank 1 for the highest–scoring set of items to rank 6 for the lowest.

TINKER, TAILOR, SYSTEMS ANALYST...

Patterns of scores may vary in lots of different ways. You may score much higher on one or two of the interest areas than on the others. Alternatively, you may find that you seem to score highly in nearly all areas, or not score very highly in any area.

Before we go on to explore the meaning of this interests profile, let's complete another exercise. This is a different way of looking at the same six types of work activity.

Exercise 3: preference for work activities

The purpose of this exercise is to examine your preferences for the six types of work activity.

Circle the type of activity you prefer in each pair:

Practical	Creative	Social
or	*or*	*or*
Creative	Social	Administrative

Social	Entrepreneurial	Intellectual
or	*or*	*or*
Entrepreneurial	Intellectual	Social

Intellectual	Administrative	Practical
or	*or*	*or*
Administrative	Practical	Intellectual
Practical	Creative	Entrepreneurial
or	*or*	*or*
Social	Intellectual	Administrative
Creative	Entrepreneurial	Administrative
or	*or*	*or*
Entrepreneurial	Practical	Creative

Count up the number of times you have circled each type of activity and record the scores in your notebook. The maximum possible score for each type is 5. When you add all the scores together they should total 15.

Now compare the three highest-scoring activity areas in the two exercises:

	Exercise 2	**Exercise 3**
Highest		
Second		
Third		

What do the results of the two exercises show? Have you identified the same work interest areas in both exercises as being of most importance to you?

Do your results show that you have one or two particularly strong areas of interest, or are several of your scores from these exercises similar?

If you have clearly identified a preference for one or two interest areas you should find it easier to make career decisions because you have well-formed preferences about the sort of work that will interest you.

On the other hand, if your interests seem to be in several different areas, it may be that you will need to do some research about jobs and how they differ before you can tell where your specific interests lie.

It may be that you have been put off a certain area of work by a bad experience – for example, an unsympathetic boss – or from trying to do a job without the necessary training.

You also need to find out whether your interests seem to be pointing you towards one single part of the map or to several different parts. You can find this out by going back to the diagram (on page 20) which shows how the six interest areas relate to the two axes, people – things and data – ideas. Are the two interest areas for which you have the strongest preference for alongside each other in this diagram?

If they are, this suggests that the sort of jobs that are available in this area will offer you opportunities for interesting work.

If you find that your interests are in areas which are not alongside each other in the diagram, this suggests that you may have to look more widely at jobs from the two or more areas that might interest you. However, many jobs can satisfy more than one area of interest. Frequently, you can identify a type of work that satisfies your strongest area of interest but choose to pursue it in an environment or work setting that will satisfy your other area of interest. In this way you could work alongside people doing different jobs but who have similar interests. For example, working as a secretary in an advertising agency or a social services department is likely to offer very different kinds of work colleagues.

Are you where you want to be?

By completing the two exercises you should have identified the sort of activities you would enjoy in your work. Now ask yourself whether your present job (or alternatively your last job) contained these sort of activities.

The easiest way to do this is to repeat Exercise 2, only this time ask yourself as you complete it: 'Does my current [last] job involve . . . ?

How does your current or last job compare with your preferences? Does it offer you the sort of activities that you enjoy?

If it does, this does not necessarily mean that you should not be reviewing your career plans or even looking for a job change, but it should reassure you that you are already in the right area of the map of work interests. This is likely to help in your planning, because you are more likely to know about jobs similar to your present one.

If your current or last job does not offer activities that are important to you or offers only some of them, this is one important reason for reviewing your career plans.

By identifying the sort of activities you enjoy, you have now identified where you want to be on the map of work interests in an ideal world. You should now be in a strong position to review your skills, knowledge and experience to see whether you are equipped for the sort of work opportunities that are available there.

Summary

We have spent today:

- learning about the key dimensions of work interests
- reviewing the work activities that you enjoy
- considering the extent to which your current or last job satisfies your work interests

What are you good at?

Having thought about where your job interests lie, you now need to move on to think about your skills, knowledge and experience. This means both being aware of why you need to assess yourself as well as having some techniques for carrying out this assessment. This requires:

- understanding the need for self-assessment
- using exercises to review your skills and experience
- deciding whether you like what you are good at

In thinking about what you are good at, it is important not just to think about what you do in your present job but also to include what you have done in previous jobs and outside of paid work.

Understanding the need for self-assessment

If we were concerned with selecting someone for a job, we would want to assure ourselves that they were capable of

doing it. What sort of evidence of their ability to do the job would we consider relevant?

Almost certainly we would want evidence of the kind of work they had done previously. This would help us determine whether they were likely to have the skills, knowledge and experience required for the job. We might also want to know about their educational qualifications. Educational qualifications give both a broad indication of overall level of ability and show whether someone has the specific skills and knowledge required for certain types of work.

The weight given to each of these components will vary considerably for different sorts of jobs. Qualifications are important for technical and professional jobs; they may be less important for non-technical and managerial jobs, where skills and experience are the main indicators of suitability. Selectors will also give more weight to recent work history than to qualifications that were gained many years ago.

It is just the same for you when trying to determine whether you are qualified to do certain sorts of job. You have to review your skills, knowledge and experience, as well as your educational qualifications, to work out what sort of jobs you may be capable of doing.

Assessing skills and experience

Of course, you are not yet at the stage of being selected for a job. Rather, you are trying to work out what jobs you might be able to do. *How are you going to do this?*

Answer 1: using your expert knowledge

In some circumstances, selectors go out and measure the performance of people who are currently doing the same job elsewhere, to build up an objective picture of the skills required for job. In this process they may use tests, measures of work output (e.g. production figures), ratings of performance from managers and so on. Frequently, however, it is not possible to collect this kind of objective information. Selectors therefore have to make their own judgements about the skills, knowledge and experience that are required for the job. It is generally assumed that selectors are able to do this because of their expert knowledge.

This is what you are going do to today. You will use your expert knowledge of yourself to review the skills, knowledge and experience you have acquired throughout your life.

The strength of this approach is that no one should know you better than you know yourself. However, for this approach to be successful requires strict honesty in assessment. After all, someone who is not honest in self-assessment fools no one but themselves.

Answer 2: using exercises
The remainder of today is going to be spent in completing and interpreting two exercises. These exercises are designed to help you review your skills, knowledge and experience. The first exercise aims to give you an opportunity to make an overall assessment of your skill level, while the second one aims to generate a more detailed list of the skills, knowledge and experience you have acquired.

Of course, two short self-completion exercises do not constitute a thorough assessment of skills; the aim here is to get started on the self-assessment process and to enable you to see in what broad areas you feel you have skills. Several of the works in the Guide to resources at the back of the book contain additional exercises that can be used to give a more detailed assessment.

Exercise 4: identifying your areas of strength

This exercise asks you to judge how your skills compare with those of other people. Think about your skills in relation to the four compass points of our work map:

People: work skills involved in working with people might include managing and organising people, persuading and negotiating with people, supporting and giving help to people, teaching, entertaining or understanding other people.

Things: work skills involved in making or constructing things might include the manual skills in using tools and working with machinery, the ability to understand how things work, having good hand–eye coordination.

Data: work skills involved in handling information might include interpreting a graph, working with figures on a computer, deciding how best to present and communicate information.

Ideas: work skills associated with being creative might include designing or adapting things, improvising, being innovative, having an interest in ideas and how to develop them, experimenting and investigating.

First of all, rate yourself in comparison to people in general. Compared to other people, how good are you at working with people, things, data and ideas? Circle the appropriate phrase in each case:

People
Excellent   Very good   Quite good   Not very good   No good at all

Things
Excellent   Very good   Quite good   Not very good   No good at all

Data
Excellent   Very good   Quite good   Not very good   No good at all

Ideas
Excellent   Very good   Quite good   Not very good   No good at all

How do you rate yourself? Have you given yourself a similar rating for each of the four skill areas, or do you think that you have a higher level of skills in some areas than in others?

Next, try rating yourself again, only this time making your comparisons in terms of people doing the sort of jobs in which you are interested.

These are your self-ratings of your skills. They are a measure of how you see your skills in relation to those of other people.

How accurate are these judgements? One way of testing this is to get someone else who knows you well to rate you in these four skill areas. Some of us are modest and tend to underestimate our skills, while others of us are more generous in the way we rate ourselves. Getting a second opinion is one way of finding out whether our perceptions match those of others (friends, work colleagues, or family).

The next exercise aims to review in more detail your skills, knowledge and experience.

Exercise 5: reviewing your skills, knowledge and experience

The only way to do this is to review things you have already done and to think hard about what they involved. This exercise uses the same four headings as in Exercise 4; this makes it easy to look at the results of both exercises together. This exercise needs to be done in several stages.

The first step is to think of things you have done: for example, your current job (if you have one), a previous job that you liked, a previous job that you disliked, something you have carried out (a serious hobby or outside interest), a role you have experienced (parent, student). There is no limit to the number that can be listed. Try to list two or three to start with.

Next, you need to identify the activities that were involved in the jobs or roles that you have listed. Write some of the activities that make up each job or role on a new page of your notebook. Looking at these activities will help you identify the skills, knowledge and experience you have used.

Now, using a fresh page, write at the top the name of the job or role you are reviewing then write down the left-hand side the three headings, *Skills, Knowledge, Experience*, equally spaced down the sheet. You will need a new page like this for each job/role you examine.

Now try to list the *skills* that are associated with each of the activities that you have listed for each job or role.

You will need to ask yourself these kinds of questions for each job or role:

Did you work with people? If so, in what way? Persuading them or selling something to them? Teaching or training them? Was leadership involved?

Did you work with things? What sort of things? Machines or tools? Working out how to make something? Were physical skills, like hand-eye coordination, important?

Did you work with data? How? Did you have to organise or administer it? Were you collating information or figures? Were financial skills involved? Was attention to detail important?

Did you work with ideas? Were you creating something? Did this include designing something? Researching or finding out about it?

Next list the *knowledge* that you used when carrying out the activities in each job or role.

Did you have relevant educational, academic or professional qualifications? What knowledge did you acquire from doing this job/role?

Third, list the *experience* you gained from doing this job/role. Did you work as part of a team or on your own? What special experience do you associate with this job/role? Was there anything you really disliked about it?

Before the final part of the exercise, make several copies of the form opposite. One copy can then be completed for each of your roles.

Having written your entries under the three headings *Skills, Knowledge, Experience*, you can then go on to classify them under the four headings *People, Things, Data, Ideas*, and write them onto one of your forms.

Once you have completed one job or role, repeat the process for the second one, and so on.

	PEOPLE	THINGS	DATA	IDEAS
SKILLS				
KNOWLEDGE				
EXPERIENCE				

Putting it all together

The final stage of the exercise is to go through all your completed forms and look at what you have listed. For each entry, whether it is under skills, knowledge or experience, you must decide whether you were good at it.

Now make another copy of the master form and summarise, in the appropriate box, the things that you are good at.

Making sense of all this

You should now be in a position to review what you have learned about yourself.

First of all, can you see any pattern in skills, knowledge and experience you have acquired? Have some things come up several times? Are they in the same categories?

Are you good at them? Is there a pattern in the things you are good at? What are you *really* good at?

Looking at this list of things you are good at, it is now appropriate to ask yourself: Do you like doing these things? Of these, which ones are really important to you? Which ones would you like to do more?

Linking skills to jobs

As well as the very detailed profile you have now built up about yourself, you also need to be able to summarise where you think you should be located on the map of work types.

Look at the 'wheel' diagram on this page. Colour, tick or mark in some other way the sectors of the wheel where you now know you have skills, knowledge or experience. The areas can be related to the results from Monday's exercises on work interests.

Check back with Exercise 4. Do the results of the two exercises agree? Having completed Exercise 5, do you want to change the way you have rated yourself on Exercise 4?

Are your skills in:

- adjacent sectors?
- opposite sectors?
- more than half the sectors?

Are your areas of strength the same as your areas of interest?

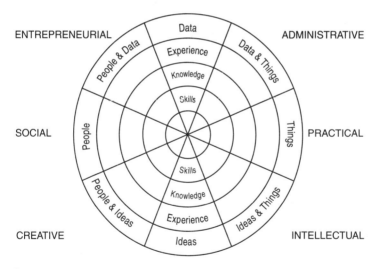

Summary

We have spent Tuesday reviewing what you are good at. We have set out to:

- understand why you need to do this
- review your skills, knowledge and experience
- see how they relate to the four areas of data, ideas, people and things
- map out these areas

Identifying your career options

You have started the career planning process by learning about yourself: examining your own values, interests, skills, knowledge and experience. Now it is time to turn to the second major building block of the career planning framework: learning about jobs. We will spread this task over the next two days. Today, we start by thinking as widely as possible about career options.

You may find that some career options which look exciting turn out to be less attractive or less achievable when you know more about them. You may need to go through the process of generating options and researching them several times before you move on to make a career action plan.

Today we will examine:

- what is happening to jobs and careers
- what kinds of jobs there are
- your own career options

What is happening to jobs and careers?

In thinking about our own career options, it is important to bear in mind general trends in the world of work. The job market is always in a state of change and this turbulence has been increasing over the last 20 years.

The economy
The state of the economy clearly affects our job options. In a recession, opportunities are likely to be in short supply. In a period of rapid economic growth, there are more job

vacancies. These are not caused just by new jobs, but also by people moving more freely from job to job. It will be easier at such times to re-enter the labour market or make radical career moves.

Also, the job market varies between sectors of the economy and parts of the country. Some types of employer can be recruiting while others are reducing numbers.

The media report such economic information, often mentioning aspects of the job market. We should use this knowledge to decide the tactics of our job moves. Given the turbulence of economic conditions, however, we should not let short-term economic changes dominate our longer-term career strategy.

Longer-term changes in jobs and careers
More important to longer-term career options are underlying shifts in the employment structure. These vary in detail by country, region and sector, but some broad shifts are apparent in most Western nations:

- a reduction of employment in so-called primary sectors: agriculture, fishing, mining, etc.
- relatively fewer jobs in manufacturing industry
- relatively more jobs in the service sectors, e.g. retailing, financial services, health and personal services
- an increase in the relative importance of employment in smaller organisations and of self-employment
- the 'contracting out' of some work from larger organisations (e.g. in security, catering, cleaning) to smaller organisations or the self-employed

- a growth in temporary and part-time employment
- a decline in less skilled jobs and a growth in high-skill, professional and 'knowledge' jobs

These changes have resulted in significant levels of general unemployment, coexisting with shortages of people with particular skills.

These shifts in employment, plus alterations to the way large organisations operate, have also changed careers:

- a 'job for life' is not now a realistic expectation; most people need to be prepared for several changes in occupation during their working lives, and many more changes in job
- flatter organisation structures mean more of us will have to find sideways rather than vertical career moves

- large organisations now expect their employees to manage their own career moves and skill development

Managing our own career

To manage our own careers, we need to develop new skills such as:

- flexibility and adaptability
- ability to learn new skills, especially higher-level and technological skills
- willingness and ability to manage our own career and skill development
- collecting and interpreting labour market information

Kinds of jobs

Most of us are restricted in our career planning by our very limited knowledge of the jobs that exist. We know about the jobs that our parents, friends and teachers do or tell us about. There are many jobs we never consider because we do not know about them. So how do we start thinking about jobs?

A useful starting point is to take the same concepts we used on Monday to map work interests. We can look at jobs in terms of whether they predominantly involve working with people, things, data or ideas.

We used six headings to think about activities and interests, and the same categories can be used again to think about broad 'families' of jobs, as follows:

- 'entrepreneurial': business and management jobs
- 'administrative' or organisational jobs
- 'practical' or technical jobs
- 'intellectual': scientific and research jobs
- 'creative' and artistic jobs
- 'social' and personal services jobs

Within each family there are jobs at various levels, in various sectors and with a range of specific content. A few illustrations might help your imagination to get going. While reading this section, keep a note of any jobs which seem worth exploring.

Entrepreneurial jobs include: jobs in business and management, marketing and selling such as telephone sales, marketing manager, retail manager, shop assistant, buyer, personnel manager, estate agent.

Administrative and organisational jobs include: clerical, secretarial and administrative jobs, jobs in finance, actuaries, tax consultants, management accountants.

Practical and technical jobs include: a vast number of jobs working with different materials and technologies and at a wide range of levels, from labourers to nuclear engineers, such as jobs in construction (building trades, surveyor, etc.), in manufacturing (operators, technicians etc.), in transport, engineering, leisure (domestic staff, chef), agriculture and horticulture (gardener, tree surgeon, vet).

Intellectual jobs include: jobs in research, science, medicine and social sciences, such as laboratory technician, geologist, statistician, radiographer, nutritionist, surgeon, economist, maths teacher.

Creative and artistic jobs include: music, dance, theatre and the visual arts, director, producer, journalist, professional sport, advertising, fashion work, architecture and design, photography.

Social and personal service jobs include: playleader, teacher, lecturer, social worker, counsellor, hotel receptionist, air steward/stewardess, beauty therapist, prison officer.

Of course, there are jobs which combine elements of more than one family. For example, technical jobs in the arts – theatrical electrician, sound technician – combine creative with technical skills. Many jobs in health and the law – nurse, barrister – combine personal and scientific or research skills.

Identifying career options

Now it is time to generate your own list of career options. It is important that at this stage you think as widely – even wildly – as possible. Even if you eventually decide to stick with the same job, or a very similar one, such exploration will reassure you that you *are* in the right line of work, at least for now.

Types of career options
You can think about your career options in terms of how far away they are from what you are doing now, or did most recently when you were last at work.

Types of options might include:

- changing the content of your current job
- moving to a job for which you have the skills
- moving to a job requiring some further training or job experiences
- making a major career change into a new area of work, often requiring new qualifications

- other changes, e.g. taking a break from work, voluntary work, going back into full-time education, becoming self-employed, etc.

Generating a list of options

There is no single best way to approach this task. You may already have several options in mind; or you may be starting with a blank sheet of paper.

Here are some of the starting points you could use in listing your own career options. Jot down any ideas that come to mind as you think.

- Do some of the 'families' of jobs described above excite you or contain jobs you have always wanted to do? Look back at the work you have done on your values (Exercise 1), interests (Exercises 2 and 3) and skills (Exercises 4 and 5) to identify at least some job families which are likely to suit you
- If job families seem too general, some more detailed careers material contains lists of jobs within each of these families (see Guide to resources at the end of this book)
- Think about the different types of career option listed above
- Fantasise about the perfect job. What would a perfect working day consist of? What would you be doing, and in what surroundings?
- Talk to family, friends and colleagues
- Look in newspapers and journals at job advertisements

- If you are in employment, look afresh at your current job and consider whether it would meet your needs if you could change it in some way
- Think too about jobs elsewhere in your current organisation – not just promotions but also jobs in other locations, in other departments or units and in other functions or occupations

For each of your options, try to think about where your desired activities or jobs might exist. Identify:

- possible sectors, types of employer or particular organisations
- whether any options involve things other than conventional paid employment, e.g. voluntary work, self-employment, full-time study, etc.

It is important to think too about some of the implications of each option, such as money, working time, geographical location or the need to study.

Listing and summarising your career options

This part of our process should have helped you to generate several career options. You should summarise these before moving on.

Exercise 6: summarising career options

First write a simple list of each of the career options so far identified. Remember you can always come back to this list and add more options later if you choose.

For example, someone re-entering paid employment after several years caring for their young children might be considering:

- going back to teaching
- educational psychology
- some form of self-employment – perhaps writing

A young graduate accountant might include:

- gaining faster promotion to partner
- moving to a larger company
- finance work in another sector, perhaps retail
- doing something quite different once qualified: taking a management course, travelling

Now you need to complete a summary sheet for each of your options, recording the most important things about it. A sample format for this summary is shown opposite.

Career option summary

Name/title for this option:

Type of option (*circle one or add own classification*):
- changing content of your current job
- moving to a job for which you have the skills
- moving to a job requiring training/experience
- a major career change
- other

Job family, job activities or occupations involved
(*including possible jobs if known*):

Possible employer or job context (*particular employers or types of employer, voluntary work, self-employed, full-time education etc.*):

Implications of this option (*finance, patterns of work, location, requirements for education or training*):

Attractions of this option:

Summary

We have spent Wednesday considering:

- what is happening to jobs and careers
- what types of jobs there are
- your own career options

Collecting information

Now you have drawn up a list of career options, how do you move towards an action plan? It is tempting to move straight to choosing an option or applying for jobs. It is also unwise. We usually need to know a good deal more about each of our options before we are in a position to make judgements about them. This phase of 'active job research' makes all the difference between good career decisions and poor ones.

Today you need to turn from a dreamer into a detective. Your elusive quarry will be the real job. Only when you have a good understanding of what each of your options really involves can you make a wise choice.

We will be examining:

- your information needs
- career paths
- sources of information on careers and jobs
- using information interviews

Your information needs

There are three main sets of questions you need to answer when you are researching jobs:

What would this option really be like?

- In what environment would you be working?
- What would you be doing?
- Likely conditions of employment

What would you need?

- What skills are required?
- What knowledge or qualifications are required?
- What previous experience is required?

Will there be opportunities available?

Once you have the answers to these questions, then you can compare them with your own values, interests, skills, knowledge and experience to decide which options will suit you best.

The same questions can be applied to career options which are not just job moves. For example, if you are considering self-employment you can ask yourself what that change will really mean for you, what skills you will need, and whether you can create a realistic opportunity for yourself.

Exercise 7: career option research

This exercise goes a step further from the brief description of each option you generated yesterday. The blank form shows some headings you might use for each option to structure the information you collect. The notes on the headings suggest some of the specific things you should be finding out.

Career Option Research
Name/title of career option

What would this option really be like?
Work environment (*employers, values, environment*):

Job content (*role, level, responsibilities, activities*):

Conditions of employment (*pay, hours, etc.*):

Requirements for this option
Skills/knowledge:

Qualifications:

Previous job/career experience:

Likely levels of opportunity

Work environment matters as well as the content of a job, and choosing an environment which is compatible with your work values can be crucial. From a practical point of view, you need to find out who your likely employers might be. You also need to know with what sorts of people you will be working, the physical environment you can expect, and the culture of the organisation. Later on, these items will tell you to what extent each option is compatible with your personal values.

Job content is of paramount importance, including:

- What is this job there to do (job role) and how does it fit into the organisation?
- If the job exists at more than one level, into which job levels might you fit, perhaps in both the short and the longer term?
- What are job holders' responsibilities?
- What would a typical working day involve?
- How predictable is the work? Is it stressful? How much freedom and autonomy do job holders have?

Conditions of employment cover the financial and domestic implications of each option, e.g. pay, benefits, pensions, costs of education courses, working hours and patterns, travelling or working away from home, possible relocation.

Work environment, job content and conditions of employment tell you what each career option would really feel like. They apply just as much to full-time education or self-employment as to conventional jobs.

Skills and knowledge requirements tell us:

- what we have to be able to do
- what we have to know about

You will be using this information later to assess your suitability for each option, and your likely training and education needs.

It is often possible to extrapolate from job activities to the skills and knowledge required. For example, the school-teacher thinking of writing educational materials would have to get ideas accepted by publishers, research, design and write. Skills required would include imagination, persuasion, negotiation, research, writing at the right level, and time management. Knowledge of the market would also be critical to success.

Formal *qualifications* are used by employers as another 'filter' for applicants. For some jobs, including many professions, they are a statutory requirement. You will need to find out which qualifications are necessary or preferred for your chosen option.

There is a rough association between job level and level of qualifications required:

- *no formal qualifications*: mainly unskilled and semi-skilled jobs
- *general qualifications from school*: many clerical and craft jobs, often followed by specific vocational training
- *higher-level qualifications*: many jobs require good school-leaving qualifications plus specific training, but not a degree
- *degree or professional qualifications*: most specialist jobs and, increasingly, management

Skills and knowledge are what we need to do a job, but employers often use what we have done before – our *previous job/career experience* – as an indicator of these. In many walks of life there are jobs which are difficult to enter without having done some of the activities before, often at a more junior level. Sometimes you may be able to convince an employer to take a chance on you, even if you do not have the usual background experience. However, you still should arm yourself with the knowledge of what previous experience is normally expected. You need to know:

- the types of jobs and job levels at which you can enter your desired organisation or occupation
- the subsequent sequences of job experience – career paths – which are most often followed
- the range of experience expected for your desired job

Mapping career paths

If you find the career paths hard to think about for any of your particular options, it can help to try and map them. This is especially helpful for options which involve quite a few job or training steps between where you are now and where you want to be. Career path maps can be drawn for an occupation (e.g. entering educational psychology as a new career) or for more specific options within a given employer (e.g. the young accountant wanting to make his way to a partnership).

Exercise 8: drawing a career path map

Try drawing a map for some of your options which involve several job steps. Show boxes for relevant types of job experience. Put more junior jobs lower down on the page and more senior jobs higher up, with job levels in different work areas roughly lined up across the page. Arrows show career moves between boxes, which may involve a change in:

- level or job role
- department, unit or location
- function (e.g. production, personnel, sales etc)
- employer

If you are trying to enter an organisation, you should mark the jobs where external recruitment occurs.

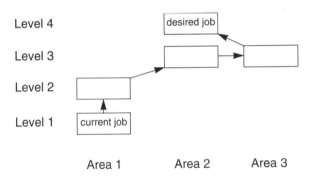

The typical career map shown here illustrates a career option involving a desired job type three levels above the current job (these may be from trainee, to qualified, to supervisor, to manager). It also shows moving to an area of work (Area 2) different from the current one (Area 1). To achieve this, it may be necessary to gain experience in a third area (Area 3).

These areas of work may be functions (production, finance, sales, etc.), different parts of the same function, different units (factory, head office) or different locations (a small-town bank, a large city branch, an overseas operation, etc.). They might also represent different employers. Often the map will show more than one possible route to where you want to get.

You can use these maps to identify more clearly short- and longer-term job goals.

Likely levels of opportunity
We have already discussed changing employment patterns and the labour shortages and surpluses they bring. It is important to be aware of which career options will offer plenty of opportunity and which will be very competitive.

High levels of opportunity are found in:

- new or rapidly growing areas of activity or new technologies
- occupations for which few people have been training, and where shortages may develop
- occupations from which many people are about to retire, and where replacements will be needed

Your job research should ask:

- Is the number of jobs growing or shrinking?
- How many vacancies exist at present?
- Are there large numbers of applicants?
- Do opportunities vary geographically or from one employer to another?
- Are you likely to face particular barriers in pursuing this option because of age, gender, race, disability, etc.?

Information sources

Your information needs will be quite wide ranging, but there are many sources of job information. The process itself can be fun and interesting. Your main access to job information will be through:

- people you know
- external information sources
- information within your own organisation
- people doing the job – through information interviews

People you know (colleagues, friends and family) may know about the job you have in mind, or have a friend who does. They may know about the organisation you are considering, or the college course you might take. It is always better to talk to someone who has had real contact with a job, rather than just listen to general opinions. If you know 100 people, and they each know 100 people, that gives you 10 000 people to ask – assuming you all have different friends!

External information sources include:

- brochures and reports from potential employers
- press and journals: job advertisements and articles on job and career trends
- reference books, career directories and reference material, available in public libraries
- careers services and educational institutions
- recruitment agencies
- industry and professional bodies: these often produce the most comprehensive information both on careers and on qualifications required
- trade unions and employee organisations

Information within your own organisation can be very useful if you are currently employed and considering career options within the same organisation. However, make careful judgements about whom you talk to and when. Choose people who will keep a confidence if asked to.

There are many other internal information sources:

- business information, e.g. annual reports, newsletters, business plans or objectives, is usually freely available
- job vacancies are often put on notice-boards
- the personnel function usually holds information on jobs, e.g. recruitment literature, training schemes, organisation charts, job descriptions, skill and qualifications requirements
- some employers have special libraries containing information on careers and training

- successful people in the job area you have in mind provide useful clues as to what career paths are valued, and what skills are required
- senior people are often happy to advise or take a 'mentoring' role (your own manager can be a useful ally) but should be asked for information with care and not approached early if they are likely to block your efforts

Once you have done some preparatory research it can be extremely valuable to talk to someone who actually does the job you have in mind. We call this an *information interview* .

Information interviews do not just help your research. They also give you a chance to meet people who might be willing to help you later on, or to recommend other useful contacts.

UH-HUH – THAT'S FROM MY PERSONAL EXPERIENCE

When conducting an information interview:

- explain that the purpose of the interview is to help you find out more about a type of job in which you are interested
- prepare in advance what you are going to say and ask
- take good notes
- keep it short
- be pleasant and not too pushy, but take a CV with you just in case
- send a thank-you letter
- treat other contacts you may be given with discretion

Exercise 9: the information interview

Try out an information interview. Practise the technique on a friend or colleague first if you wish. Some questions to ask include:

- What does the job involve on a day-to-day basis?
- Where does it fit in with the rest of the organisation?
- Are there significant changes going on in the job or the organisation?
- What skills are most important in the job?
- Are any qualifications required/preferred?
- What are the career backgrounds of job holders?
- Are there likely to be vacancies in future?

Summary

Today you have researched your career options by:

- defining your information needs
- mapping possible career paths
- identifying information sources
- using information interviews

Now we have completed the second building block of career planning – understanding jobs. We are now ready to go on to the third and final stage of career planning – making a choice and taking action.

Remember if you are not happy with any of the career options you have generated so far, you can go back to the options thinking stage and try again.

Making a choice

The main task for today is to pull together what you have
learnt so far this week. You need to examine how the career
options you have researched measure up with your values
and interests and whether they meet your personal
requirements. You also need to consider how well your
skills, knowledge and experience match up with those
demanded by your options, and whether opportunities are
likely to be available.

By the end of today you should have a firm sense of
direction, so that you can move on to taking action. This
means that there are a number of important questions that
you must try to answer today. Most importantly, you must
try to decide whether you have identified a career option
that is both *attractive* and *achievable*.

Many career plans will involve skill development, and in the final part of this chapter, we will review how to go about accessing development opportunities at work or through education.

Pulling together what you have found out

By now you should have identified several possible career options and researched them in some depth. The stages in deciding between those various options involve:

- deciding how attractive each option is to you by comparing your options with your work values and work interests
- reviewing the impact of any factors that may constrain your choice of options
- deciding how achievable each option is for you by comparing your options with your skills, knowledge and experience, and levels of opportunity
- determining your overall preference between options

Start by trying to decide which option is most attractive to you. First, gauge the extent to which each option matches up with your work values.

Comparing options with your work values
One way to do this is to review each of your options against your self-rating of work values (Exercise 1). Consider the three work values that you identified as most important and ask for each of your possible career options:

Will the work involve this value? (Answer YES or NO)

How does each option score? It is worth rating your current job as well (if you have one).

Now repeat the exercise, only this time consider the three work values that you identified as least important, the values you ranked eighth, ninth and tenth.

How do the options compare? Will they provide opportunities for you to experience what is important to you?

If your options involve values that are not important to you, it may not matter. For example, the fact that an option is likely to provide a high salary or a friendly work environment is not going to put most of us off. However, you may be trying to avoid work that involves certain work values – risk, for example.

Comparing options with your work interests
You have already identified your profile of work interests.
Now you need to see whether your possible options are
likely to involve activities that interest you. If you have
researched your options thoroughly you will now know
something about what they involve.

One way to do this is to construct a profile for each of your
options in just the same way that you constructed a profile
for yourself. You can do this by going back to Exercise 2,
where you rated yourself, and using the same framework to
rate each option in turn.

For each option, ask the question:

Does this option provide opportunities for . . .?

Use the 1 to 5 scale giving scores from 1 for an option that
will provide no opportunity for this activity to 5 for an
option that will provide plenty of opportunity for this
activity.

Now you can compare your own score profile with that of
each of your options. Some key questions are:

- Are the two highest activity areas for each of your
  options the same as or different from those that you
  found you preferred?
- Are all your possible options scoring highly in the
  same interest areas?
- How do your options compare with your current job?

What do you learn from this? How attractive are your
options to you? Are they the sorts of jobs that you would
enjoy? How do they match up with your real priorities?

At this stage you may be in one of three different situations.

1 Options match interests and values.
You are ready to go on and see how you measure up against your options in terms of skills, knowledge and experience.

2 Options match interests and values to some extent.
Should you go back and review your options? Can you think of any other options that you ought to consider? Or have you changed your mind about your interests and values?

3 Options do not seem to match up with interests and values.
More work is required. Review your values and interests. You may also want to review your options. It may be helpful to ask someone else for a second opinion (friends, work colleagues, family). You should not expect to make your career plan on your own, so this may be a good time to involve someone else.

It is possible that you are not yet ready to make a career plan. You may need to do more work on the first two building blocks of the career planning process – *learning about self* or *learning about jobs*. See the Guide to resources at the back of the book for additional sources of information. This includes work books that can be used to help in learning about yourself as well as additional sources of occupational information.

Practical constraints
In assessing the overall attractiveness of different options, remember the practical constraints on your work choices, which we looked at on Thursday.

- *Working patterns* – How much time do you wish to give to your work? Are you constrained by domestic and caring responsibilities, or other activities and interests? For example, do you wish to work part time or term time only?
- *Work location* – How far are you prepared to travel to work? Are you willing to move house? Would you like to work from home?
- *Pay and benefits* – Will your requirements for pay and other benefits be met?

'BYE DEAR. SEE YOU THIS EVENING

Comparing options with your skills, knowledge and experience
A key purpose of our research into possible options has been to find out their demands in terms of skills, knowledge and experience. You should now be able to use the information generated about your skills, knowledge and experience to determine how well you match with each of your possible options.

For most types of career option, you will find yourself in one of three situations.

1 *You already have the skills, knowledge and experience required.*

If so, you are ready to go forward with action planning.

2 *You have most of the skills, knowledge and experience required.*

If you are in this position, the next stage may be to review carefully how you might acquire the small amount of additional skills, knowledge and experience that you think you require.

3 *You currently lack the skills, knowledge and experience required.*

You may need to go back and look at the results of Exercises 5 and 7 to remind yourself whether the skills and knowledge that you currently possess match up with those of your job options.

Skills and knowledge are often acquired through education. You should have found out whether there are qualifications that people doing these jobs are expected to possess. *Do you possess them or are you about to possess them?*

Are there other skills or knowledge that are necessary to do this job? Can you provide evidence that you have acquired these skills and/or the relevant knowledge?

Do you have the necessary experience to convince someone that you can do the job? Do you feel you have the experience, but would find it difficult to convince someone that it is really relevant? Alternatively, should you be thinking about how you are going to get the experience?

The next stage is to review the possibilities for acquiring the skills, knowledge and experience that you need before you can pursue your desired job option.

If you have the skills, knowledge and experience, then your action planning is more about how you can market yourself appropriately.

If you do not feel you have all that is required, one component of your action planning is going to be about how to acquire what you are missing.

This may mean some more research to find out how people acquire the sort of experience you feel you require. What jobs do they do? Can you get one of those jobs?

You may think that even though you do not have all the skills, knowledge and experience required for the job option you have in mind, it is still worthwhile to go ahead with your action planning, *on the assumption that you believe you can access the development you need.* The issue of access to development is considered in the later sections of this chapter.

Comparing options with likely levels of opportunity
Using the labour market information you have collected, you now need to make a judgement about the likely level of opportunity to pursue each option.

At this stage, try to make an overall judgement between the different options you have been considering. The next exercise aims to help you to make a final choice between your different options. Ideally, there should be a perfect match between your preferred option and yourself. In practice, you may have to compromise.

Your decision should be based on the extent to which
options:

- cater for your interests, values and constraints
- are within reach of your skills, knowledge and
  experience
- have sufficient levels of opportunity

Exercise 10: preferences between career options
You may find it helpful to rate each of your career options
on the following scales:

Attractiveness   Ideal

   Values   0   10

   Interests   0   10

   Constraints   0   10

Achievability

Skills	0	10
Knowledge	0	10
Experience	0	10
Opportunities	0	10
Overall rating	0	10

- How do your options compare?
- Do you have a preference for one option?
- Which option presents the best combination in terms of attractiveness and your ability to achieve it?

Accessing development

Your preferred career option may be in itself a return to full-time education or training; in this case you will have already started thinking about possible courses. However, the need for further skill development is common to many career plans. Development may involve:

- an educational course (full time or part time)
- training at work (through on-the-job coaching or training courses)
- a job move which gives you the experience you require to get closer to your career goal

In this section we look at how to access development, in the form of both educational courses and development at work.

Educational courses
In many ways going back to education is getting easier. The range of colleges and courses is expanding, and prospectuses (now seen as 'marketing' material) are easily available. There has also been a rapid growth in part-time courses, and courses taken from home (through so-called 'distance learning'). However, competition for places on some courses is stiff, fees can be high and financial help is not always available. Educational qualifications cannot guarantee you the job you want, although the right qualification will improve your chances of success.

Before choosing a course, you will need to identify what *level of qualification* might be appropriate. On Thursday we related levels of qualifications to levels of jobs. We can think of levels in terms of academic qualifications (GCSE, A level, degree, professional qualification) but there are also many vocational qualifications. In the UK a unified system of

classifying qualifications by broad level is being introduced:
National Vocational Qualifications (NVQs) and General
Vocational Qualifications (GNVQs). Colleges and employers
can advise you on the appropriate level of course to aim for.

Other aspects of courses to clarify are:

- subject or subject mix, curriculum and options
- location of colleges/distance learning options
- full-time or part-time options
- entry qualifications required
- precise qualification awarded
- recognition of course, if relevant, by professional body or employers
- length of course
- opportunities to gain work experience, e.g. placements, block releases
- facility to change course if desired
- fees and availability of grants/sponsorship
- special government or industry schemes
- pattern of terms and hours of attendance
- teaching methods and staff/student ratios
- methods of assessment (exam, coursework, etc.)

Career development processes at work

Most of the development we gain in our working lives
happens on the job or near to it. Your job research may have
already given you clear ideas about job moves you need to
make for development reasons. However, development at
work will not just fall into your lap. You will need to
understand the processes used by employers to develop
their staff, and learn to use those processes to gain access to
the training and job moves you need.

Personnel management has its own jargon and the diagram below shows some of the processes we should try and find out about. We need to know:

- what each process is used for: how it affects the jobs people get and the training they receive
- whether we can use the process to obtain career information, send signals to the organisation about what we want to do or have a better dialogue about possible options

Four important types of use shown in the diagram are: *assessment, job-filling, development* and *career planning*. Processes can have more than one use. For example, an appraisal interview can be used to assess (openly or secretly), to discuss career plans, and to identify training and development needs. The output of this appraisal may influence whether the person being appraised is eligible to apply for jobs and whether he or she is selected.

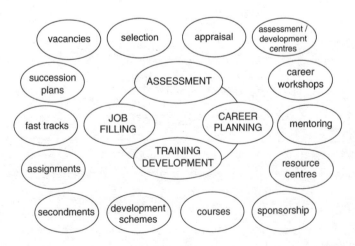

Some processes are used primarily for *assessment*: identifying our strengths and weaknesses. Appraisal of performance and/or potential by a manager is the commonest, but larger organisations may also use assessment centres. These consist of a series of tests, exercises and interviews applied to a group of people often over two or three days. These may act as the gateway to a particular job level (e.g. senior management) or special development programmes.

The processes for *filling jobs* are crucial but often elusive. You will need to understand how vacancies are notified, what the selection criteria are for the jobs you want, and how the selection process really takes place. If skill criteria (e.g. communications, teamworking) are specified for jobs they can give you clues to the skills you need to show you have.

A range of processes combine planned job replacement and *development*. These include development schemes or programmes, and fast tracks for 'high potential' employees. Succession plans, still usually secret, plan possible job moves for some individuals. Project assignments and secondments give valuable development. Other training and development processes include off-the-job training and facilities for sponsorship.

As the trend to self-development has taken root, newer processes, such as career workshops, are aimed at helping *career planning*. Development centres combine assessment with development planning. Learning resource centres contain career and training information. Mentoring puts employees in touch with someone more senior who can help them develop their career.

Learning to understand and play the system using these processes can be vital to us achieving our own career goals.

Summary

Today you have:

- examined your career options against your values, interests and skills.
- chosen one or more career options to form the basis of your action plan
- identified educational courses you may need
- looked at how you might use development processes at work

Taking the first steps

Now that you have settled on your preferred career option, you need to set about producing an action plan to make your vision of the future a reality. This may involve quite small changes in your current job or in your life outside work; or it may be a major upheaval including a change of job, employer and location or re-entry into education. Some action plans will therefore be quite simple while others may involve a commitment to several years of retraining and change to get to where you want to be. In either case you need to clarify and schedule your actions. Today we will be examining how these first steps are taken:

- clarifying types of action required
- preparing to present yourself through CVs, application forms and interviews
- applying for jobs and courses

- getting support
- setting goals and a timetable
- monitoring progress

Clarifying types of action required

Earlier we identified some of the main kinds of career options as:

- changing the content of your current job
- moving to a job for which you already have the skills (this could be with your current employer or elsewhere)
- moving to a job requiring further training or job experiences (again, with your current employer or elsewhere)
- making a major career change, often requiring new qualifications
- other changes, e.g. return to full-time education, self-employment, voluntary work, etc.

This way of looking at options can be helpful when you come to consider the main focus of your career action plan. Typical actions may include:

- renegotiating the content of your current job
- applying for jobs inside your own organisation
- external job search
- accessing training or development at work
- applying for educational courses
- exploring other options and changes outside work

Typical actions	Career options				
	change within job	job move	job move needing training	major career change	other options
Renegotiate present job	✓				
Internal job search		✓	✓	✓	
External job search	✓		✓	✓	
Development at work		✓	✓	✓	✓
Education			✓	✓	
Other changes				✓	✓
other changes				✓	✓

Some career options are more likely to require each of these types of action than others, as suggested by the ticks in the boxes on the action planning grid shown above. You can use this grid to think through the main focus of your action plans. Remember that changes to your life outside work can also be identified and recorded in your action plan.

Marketing yourself

One of the major hurdles in getting the sort of job you want is the selection process. This requires you to convince a potential employer that you are the right person for the job. Even if you are planning to be self-employed, you will have to convince potential customers or financiers of the viability of your venture. Essentially, you have to look at marketing yourself as though you were a product.

How do you market yourself
The first thing you must know if you are going to be successful in the job hunt is why you want the job. Primarily, this is about understanding your own motivation for applying. If you really understand your work interests and values, you will be in a good position to do this.

Second, you must be able to convince your customer, in this case your potential employer, that you have the skills that they require. Once again, the work you have already done on reviewing your skills, knowledge and experience should be of help here.

In what ways will you have to market yourself?
Almost always you will have to write about yourself. Either
you will have to fill in an application form, or you will have
to prepare a curriculum vitae (CV) that summarises your
work history.

Second, you will usually have an interview with your
potential employer. Almost everybody wants to meet
someone they will be working with. This also applies to job
moves within your current employing organisation.

Frequently, there are other components to a selection
process. For example, there may be tests and presentations
that have to be completed, or an assessment centre to attend.
You might be asked to bring along examples of your work,
or be required to provide the names of people who can give
you a reference.

It is important to realise that many selection procedures involve a number of stages, and the employer is effectively weeding out applicants at every stage of the process. This means that you must give each aspect of the selection process your best shot. There will be no second chance. Education and training providers also use similar procedures.

You should also be aware that, in general, selection procedures, particularly those used by major employers, are becoming more rigorous. There are several reasons for this. They include a greater concern for fairness, that is, not to discriminate against applicants unfairly. There is also a desire at all costs not to select people who will be unable to do the job required. The cost in time and money of running selection procedures is also an important factor for many employers.

Putting something down in writing
This is usually the first stage. Even in the most informal selection process, it will usually pay to have a curriculum vitae prepared that you can hand over.

The main difference between completing an application form and writing a CV is that with an application form it is the employer who has decided what questions to ask; with a CV you have to decide what information to present to an employer about yourself.

What should it look like? If at all possible a CV should be word-processed, or at least typed, not handwritten. One major advantage of word processing is that the CV can very easily be adapted to the particular needs of a potential employer.

The CV should be broken down into sections just like an application form. These should include:

- *Personal background information:* name, address, age, sex, etc.
- *Educational and professional qualifications:* name of school/college attended, subjects studied, highest level of qualifications obtained, dates, etc.
- *Employment history:* list of jobs (including job title, employer, dates of employment), responsibilities, key work experiences
- *Current/last job:* job title, name and address of employer, dates of employment, salary
- *Other relevant information:* e.g. achievements outside paid employment
- *Names of referees:* name, title and address for two people who would write you a reference (they should have been asked before you give details)

The exact form a CV should take will vary considerably between jobs and labour markets. If you were planning to become a university professor, your CV would list all the research you had done, the journal articles and books you had written, your teaching experiences, and so on; it might fill 20 pages. For most other jobs two or three pages will normally be sufficient.

It is usual also to include with your CV a letter or separate sheet of paper outlining your reasons for applying and emphasising which of your skills and experiences are relevant to the position. This is an opportunity to expand on the factual information contained within your CV.

You may not be able to complete some sections of a CV or an application form because, for example, you are only just leaving university and have never had a job.

Similarly, you should give less emphasis to things that happened a long time ago than to what you have done more recently, but always explain any gaps in your employment record.

Hints for application forms
Take a photocopy of the form before you begin and make detailed notes of what information you are going to put in each section, especially for open-ended questions. Fill in the photocopied version first as a draft. Ask someone else to have a look at it and only then complete the actual form.

Make a photocopy of the completed form so that you have a record of what you wrote about yourself. Check over this before you go to an interview.

Only the most skilled typists/word processor operators can 'type' an application form. The rest of us have to fill it in by hand. Pay attention to any special instructions about how to complete an application form. Does it say use black ink? (The form may well be photocopied, so black or dark blue are usually the best colours to use.) Have you written in capital letters (e.g. for surname), when requested to do so? Presentation counts for more than it used to; write neatly and check that your spelling is correct.

If you are applying for jobs where there will be hundreds of applicants, be mindful that getting any of these little details wrong might result in the rest of your application never being read. The first sift of a pile of application forms is frequently just to check that they have been completed correctly. Perhaps just 30 seconds is allocated to your form. Some applicants fail at this hurdle.

Don't lie! It may catch up with you and will almost certainly mean you lose the job. How is the employer to know that this is the only lie you have told them?

Answers to questions on application forms should always be written concisely. However, sometimes there will not be sufficient space to write in all that is relevant. In this case it is normally appropriate to use a continuation sheet. Such sheets should always have your name on, and should specify to which section of the form they apply. You may choose to write in the space on the application form, 'See separate sheet' and give all your answer on the separate sheet, or to start your answer on the form and continue on the additional sheet.

Don't leave questions unanswered; write 'None' or 'Not applicable'. Think carefully about doing this, as too many answers like this could create a negative impression.

Some application forms are now less concerned with collecting factual information and more concerned to ask for evidence about how you would cope with particular aspects of the job. For example, an application form for a sales job might ask you to describe a situation where you have coped successfully with a difficult customer.

Presenting yourself at interviews
Research and preparation are vital. This means thinking about questions you might be asked and preparing your answers. It also means thinking carefully about what information you want to be sure you get across.

If you haven't had a job interview for a long time it is a good idea to rehearse. The best way to do this is to get a friend, colleague or partner to interview you. Failing that, practise speaking your replies out loud.

Make notes of key points. Prepare possible answers for difficult questions.

Interviewers want applicants to talk; try to avoid one-word answers. *'Have you had experience of . . .'*? Answer: 'Yes, when I worked at . . . we did . . .' *or* 'No, but at . . ., we did . . .'

As well as answering the interviewer's questions, it is appropriate sometimes to add a few points about yourself that you think are especially important for the interviewer to know about.

Getting support

Once we are committed to making some changes in our
working lives – however modest – we need to discuss our
plans with other people. In some cases, for example with
friends, this has the function of helping us check out
whether our plans seems sensible to other people who know
us. We may also get help from our friends in tackling the job
market through their knowledge and networks of contacts.

When it comes to families, some career plans may simply
require their emotional support, for example in seeking a
change in the content of a current job. Other options, for
example a radical job move, a relocation or a return to
education, have profound implications for other family
members. These are clearly family decisions and need very
careful discussion.

Broaching the subject of career change at work can be quite difficult. How you deal with your manager and colleagues will depend on whether you think they are likely to be supportive and whether you need their help in moving job or accessing development.

Think too about how you can give yourself support. A major career change can be a very upsetting event to contemplate. You may feel frightened and uncertain. If you are job seeking after redundancy, or trying to return to work after a long period at home, you may face many setbacks before you achieve your goal. You need to think how to keep your spirits up and give yourself a reward for successful steps along the way.

If you are finding it very difficult to identify a satisfactory option, or to find the job you are looking for, there are other sources of support or professional help you can turn to, including:

- careers advisory services
- job clubs set up for job hunters to get together
- careers counsellors

For more information on such resources, see the Guide to resources given at the back of this book.

Setting goals and a timetable

Now it is time to try to list some of the specific goals or actions you need to take to pursue your preferred career option. This is, in essence, your career plan.

Your plan will often be a mixture of short-term and longer-term actions. For example, if the teacher we thought about earlier decides to write books from home, her list (with timetable) might include:

- sort out a small working space (this week)
- find another mother who will 'swap' childcare occasionally to cover travel in set-up phase (this month)
- map out three or four good ideas for books. Work one up in some detail (next two months)
- identify three most likely publishers and write to them (next two months)

In this case she is likely to know within a few months how feasible this plan is, and will either persist with it or adopt a different short-term goal (e.g. supply teaching) while thinking again.

The young accountant we thought about might decide to:

- give current company at most one more year to signal promotion intentions
- meanwhile make contacts in two or three larger companies expanding in Europe (six months)
- get CV up to date (this month)
- start working on his rusty French (next month)

If your plan includes looking for other jobs, then it is better to focus on making a small number of very thoughtful approaches to employers rather than sending off hundreds of standard letters. Make sure you know how these employers notify vacancies and fill jobs. Only go for jobs which really are an improvement on your current situation or take you in the direction you want to go.

If you have not changed job for a long time, you will need to allow more time for research and preparation than if you have been applying for jobs recently. In setting a timetable you should also bear in mind the amount of effort involved in each action, and when you will fit these activities in. Goals should be challenging but achievable. Discussing your goals and timescale with someone else can help you to ensure they are realistic.

Exercise 11: your career plan

Make a list of some practical goals and approximate timescales for achieving them. A simple list is more likely to help than a very complex or elaborate one.

Monitoring and adapting your plans

As with any planning process, career plans should be
frequently monitored and reviewed. Are you doing the
things you planned to do? If not, is the problem lack of
motivation or shortage of time, or do you now think that the
goal was inappropriate? Even more than other kinds of
plans, career plans must not be seen as rigid and
unchanging:

- they have no absolute timescales and direction may
  matter more than speed of progress
- they will be affected by external events and must be
  modified accordingly
- they depend wholly on your own desire for change
  and your determination not to let them fizzle out

The key is to see career planning as a learning activity. We
are learning more about the world of work and ourselves all
the time. Sometimes a setback means that a goal will be
achieved more slowly. Sometimes we learn that part of our
plan will not work out, and we need to think again and
modify our plan. Very often, our plans are conditional on
labour market opportunities, and what we continue to learn
about ourselves. For example, we often discover we have
skills we did not identify at first.

You should not, therefore, feel that you have failed if you
need to adapt your plans. What matters is that you use
career planning to give yourself a direction, and the best
chance of moving in this desired direction. As long as you
are learning in this way and acquiring skills as you go, you
are ensuring your future employability.

Career planning can be a challenging, sometimes uncomfortable, process. It can also be very hard work. However, if you don't do it, you are likely to end up at best dissatisfied and at worst unemployable. The choice is yours.

Summary

Today you have built on your earlier work of learning about jobs and about yourself. You have moved forward from your preferred career option to building a plan for action. This has included:

- types of action required
- marketing yourself through CVs, application forms and interviews
- setting goals and timescales
- monitoring and adapting plans

Guide to resources

This short list gives details of a small number of key books for further reading as well as sources of additional information.

Workbooks
Ball, B. *Manage your own Career* (1989) British Psychological Society
Hopson, B. and Scally, M. *Build your own Rainbow* (1991) Lifeskills Associates
Willis, L. and Daisley, J. *Springboard: Women's Development Workbook* (1990) Springboard

Job ideas
Miller, R. and Alston, A. *Equal Opportunities: a Careers Guide* (1988) Penguin

Job hunting
Courtis, J. *Getting a Better Job* (1993) IPM
Nelson Bolles, R. *What Color is your Parachute?* (1993) Ten Speed Press

Self-employment
Syrett, M. and Dunn, C. *Starting a Business on a Shoestring* (1988) Penguin

Careers services
Local Authority Careers Services
Careers advisory services in universities and colleges
Private careers guidance agencies
Employment Service

Further *Successful Business in a Week* **titles from** Hodder & Stoughton and the **Institute of Management all at £5.99**

All Hodder & Stoughton books are available from your local bookshop or can be ordered direct from the publisher. Just tick the titles you want and fill in the form below. Prices and availability subject to change without notice.

To: Hodder & Stoughton Ltd, Cash Sales Department, Bookpoint, 39 Milton Park, Abingdon, Oxon, OX14 4TD. If you have a credit card you may order by telephone – 01235 831700.
Please enclose a cheque or postal order made payable to Bookpoint Ltd to the value of the cover price and allow the following for postage and packaging:
UK & BFPO: £1.00 for the first book, 50p for the second book and 30p for each additional book ordered up to a maximum charge of £3.00.
OVERSEAS & EIRE: £2.00 for the first book, £1.00 for the second book and 50p for each additional book.

Name:..

Address: ....

....

If you would prefer to pay by credit card, please complete:

Please debit my Visa/Mastercard/Diner's Card/American Express (delete as appropriate) card no:

❏ ❏ ❏ ❏ ❏ ❏ ❏ ❏ ❏ ❏ ❏ ❏ ❏ ❏ ❏ ❏ ❏ ❏

Signature .... Expiry Date ....